PAST AND PRESENT

KIDNAPPING

PHILIP STEELE

new Discovery B·O·O·K·S

NEW YORK

First American publication 1992 by New Discovery Books, Macmillan Publishing Company, 866 Third Avenue, New York, NY 10022

Macmillan Publishing Company is part of the Maxwell Communication Group of Companies

First published in 1992 by Heinemann Children's Reference, a division of Heinemann Educational Books Ltd, Halley Court, Jordan Hill, Oxford OX2 8EJ

Devised and produced by Zoe Books Limited
15 Worthy Lane, Winchester, SO23 7AB, England

Edited by Charlotte Rolfe
Picture research by Faith Perkins
Designed by Julian Holland

Printed in Hong Kong

Library of Congress Cataloging-in-Publication Data

Steele, Philip
    Kidnapping / Philip Steele.
        p. cm. — (Past and present)
    Includes index.
    Summary: Examines the history of kidnapping from ancient times to the present and such related topics as ransom and the relationship of kidnapper and victim.
    ISBN 0-02-735403-2
    1. Kidnapping — Juvenile literature. [1. Kidnapping.] I. Title.
II. Series: Past and present.
HV6595.S74 1992
364.1'54 — dc20   91-42691

Photographic acknowledgments

The authors and publishers wish to acknowledge with thanks, the following photographic sources:
Camera Press pp 35; 43: Hulton Deutsch Collection pp 8; 13: Magnum title page (photographer Micha Baram): Rex Features pp 31; 34: The Royal Commonwealth Society p11: Topham Picture Source pp 4; 7; 15; 17; 19; 20; 23; 24; 27; 29; 32; 37; 38; 41.

The cover photograph is courtesy of Camera Press.

0994 DIR BKF 15.00

The publishers have made every effort to trace the copyright holders, but if they have inadvertently overlooked any, they will be pleased to make the necessary arrangement at the first opportunity.

Title page: Home at last. One of the freed passengers from an Air France plane that was seized by hijackers in 1976. The passengers were rescued from their ordeal by a commando attack which took their captors by surprise.

CONTENTS

KIDNAPPED!

A young mother is reunited with her baby at a London hospital. The newborn baby had been stolen from the hospital by a woman pretending to be a social worker.

A baby girl is snatched from her carriage outside a supermarket. A gang seizes the son of a rich banker on his way to school and demands money from his family. A journalist visiting a foreign country is captured by masked men, who refuse to release him until their demands have been met.

Wherever these events take place, we often see the frightened faces of victims and of their relatives on television. The newspapers may carry large headlines: KIDNAP PLOT FOILED or GANG DEMANDS A MILLION. We always hope that there will be a happy ending to these grim stories and that the victims will soon be reunited with their loved ones.

WHAT IS KIDNAPPING?

Individuals, and sometimes groups of people, may be **kidnapped** or "stolen" by others for many different reasons. But the act of kidnapping means they have been seized illegally, and captured and imprisoned against their own wishes.

The word "kidnap" originally meant to capture (or "nab") a child ("kid"). The term was first used in the 1670s, when many orphaned children were rounded up from the streets of English towns and sent off to work on the plantations of the new American or Caribbean colonies such as Virginia or Barbados.

Abduction is another word for kidnapping. It comes from the Latin word *abducere,* which means "to lead away." Both words are now commonly used to describe the unjust capture of any kind of person, male or female, young or old.

In 1886 the Scottish author Robert Louis Stevenson gave the title *Kidnapped* to an exciting story he had written. It told the tale of a young Scot, David Balfour, and of his adventures with a Jacobite rebel called Alan Breck. To many people the word "kidnapped" still has a romantic ring to it. It makes them imagine a world of pirates or robbers and unknown adventures.

In truth, of course, there is nothing romantic about

kidnapping. To take away a person's liberty by kidnapping him or her is one of the cruelest crimes of all. The kidnapper treats another human being simply as property that can be bought, stolen, or sold.

WHY DO PEOPLE KIDNAP?

Sometimes people commit this terrible crime simply because of greed or revenge. Some kidnappings have been carried out for other reasons, such as love, despair, or the desire for political change. In some cases, the kidnapper is a mentally ill person, acting alone, without any apparent reason.

Criminals often kidnap members of the public in order to gain a **ransom** or financial reward. They hope that relatives, companies, or other institutions will pay them a large sum of money in order to save the life of the victim. Criminals may also kidnap members of rival gangs with whom they have long-standing quarrels. They may injure or even kill their captives, hoping to frighten off their enemies in the opposing gang.

Kidnapping is a common tactic of **terrorists**. These are people who use illegal acts of violence in order to achieve political change. Terrorists may wish to frighten their enemies, or they may want to raise money in order to buy arms. By kidnapping, they may hope to bargain with a government and exchange their victims for the release of fellow terrorists from jail. Sometimes they may imprison their captives for long periods, until a suitable opportunity arises for some sort of exchange.

Governments, too, may abduct groups or individuals as an extreme way of silencing any opposition to their rule. They may use the armed forces, secret police, or criminal gangs to kidnap their opponents and then imprison or kill them. They may even kidnap individuals who have escaped to live in other countries. These people are then carried back home against their will to face jail or execution.

It is hard to believe that kidnapping can be carried

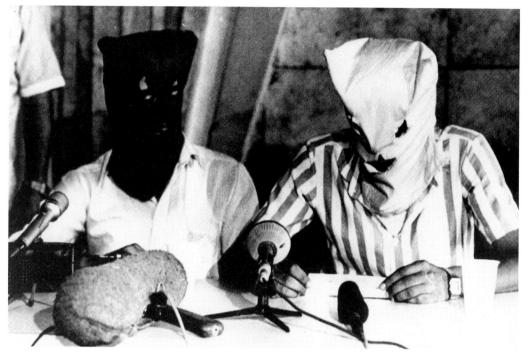

These hooded men were responsible for seizing an American TWA jet in 1985. After they had released the hostages, they held this press conference to explain their actions.

out for love, and yet today that is one of the most common reasons for child abduction. When a married couple becomes divorced, the courts may rule that any children must be brought up by one of the parents alone. Sometimes parents who may no longer see their children carry them away illegally. The newspapers have called these **tug-of-love** cases.

Sometimes a woman who has no child of her own wants one so badly that she steals one from somebody else. She may not wish to cause the child harm, but she may well do so unintentionally. Such **baby-snatchers**, as they are known, usually need treatment and help from a **psychiatrist**.

Kidnapping in all its forms may be in the news today, but it is an ancient problem that goes back long before the first use of the word.

ABDUCTION THROUGH THE AGES

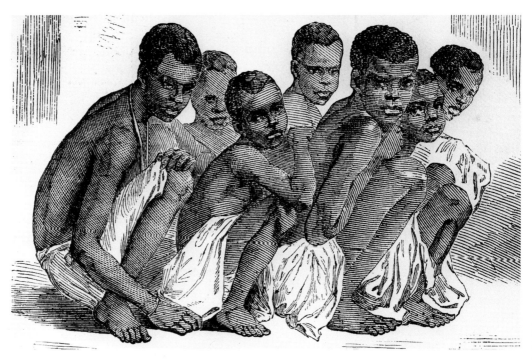

A few of the many thousands of West Africans who were kidnapped from their homes in the seventeenth and eighteenth centuries. They were sold as slave labor in the New World.

> They stole little Bridget
> For seven years long;
> When she came down again
> Her friends were all gone.
> They took her lightly back,
> Between the night and morrow,
> They thought that she was fast asleep,
> But she was dead with sorrow.
>
> *From '"The Fairies" by Irish poet William Allingham,*
> *1883*

Many ancient peoples feared that their children or loved ones would be stolen away by evil spirits, ghosts, or fairies. Stories about such things were common. In fact, the dangers of abduction were real—children who wandered away from the village could easily be seized by rival tribes. Life was hard, and every extra pair of hands could be put to work.

The story of Joseph is well known to Jews, Christians, and Muslims from their scriptures. He was seized, bound, and thrown into a pit by his brothers. He was then sold to passing merchants who led him away to slavery in Egypt. Joseph's brothers told their father, Jacob, that his favorite son had been killed by a wild animal.

THE GREEKS AND ROMANS

Abducting people for slave labor was normal in the ancient world and was not thought to be wrong. Greece and Rome depended on slaves for their everyday survival. There were perhaps 100,000 child and adult slaves in ancient Athens, making up a third of the population. Many had been kidnapped from their homes during wars, or sold by slave traders.

Roman soldiers often seized **hostages** to ensure that enemy tribes did not create trouble. One leader of the British Celts called Caractacus or Caradoc was carried off to Rome in A.D. 51. He died three years later without ever being returned to his homeland.

THE CHILDREN'S CRUSADE

In 1212 one of the greatest single mass kidnappings in history took place. It started innocently enough. Large numbers of poor children and some adults became inspired by religious enthusiasm. They vowed to go on a pilgrimage to Jerusalem in the Holy Land. They wanted to help the Crusaders, or Christian soldiers, win the city from Muslim control. About 20,000 of the young people came from the German city of Cologne. The Loire Valley in France provided another 30,000 volunteers.

The Germans walked all the way to Italy, but kidnappers were waiting for them. The girls and women were seized and forced to become household servants or **prostitutes**. The boys and young men were actually taken to the Holy Land, but there they were sold as slaves to traders from Asia. The French group fared no better. They were tricked by kidnappers in the port of Marseilles and sent to the Egyptian port of Alexandria as slaves. Two of their ships sunk at sea.

The story of these kidnapped children haunted Europe for many years. Other stories about stolen children followed, such as the legend of the Pied Piper of Hamelin. This German tale tells how a strange piper rids the town of rats in the year 1284. When he is not paid, he leads away all the children, in the same manner as the rats. They disappear into the mountainside and are never seen again.

A KING'S RANSOM

During the twelfth and thirteenth centuries the ancient practice of hostage-taking became a common practice in war. On the field of battle, ordinary soldiers were slaughtered by the thousands. However, knights and their squires, who belonged to rich or noble families, were normally captured alive. A ransom demand would then be issued.

Huge sums of money were demanded as ransom. In 1193 the English king, Richard I (known as *Cœur de*

A portrait of Olaudah Equiano, who was kidnapped from his home as a child and sold into slavery. He wrote a moving account of his experiences in *The Interesting Narrative of Olaudah Equiano*. He later regained his freedom, traveled to England, and campaigned successfully against slavery.

Lion or "Lionheart"), was kidnapped while traveling home from wars in the Holy Land. He was handed over to his enemy, the Emperor Henry VI. A ransom of 150,000 gold marks was demanded. This was never paid in full, but the amount that was paid to free him almost bankrupted England.

Less important people could be bought back for smaller sums. When the English writer Geoffrey Chaucer was captured in France in 1359, the English king paid 16 English pounds toward his release. He was duly returned home the following year.

A NEW WORLD?

In the sixteenth and seventeenth centuries, Europeans discovered new lands in Africa and America. They seized many of the peoples of these lands and sold them into slavery.

Soon the Europeans began to kidnap West Africans from settlements along the Gulf of Guinea and ship them to the Americas to work as slaves on the big plantations there. During the seventeenth century alone about 800,000 West Africans were seized from their homes. In 1755 one eleven-year-old boy, Olaudah Equiano, was kidnapped together with his sister from a village in the Essaka Valley, somewhere to the east of the Niger River. He was sold into slavery. He had many adventures and later wrote the story of his life. In it, he describes his capture by slave raiders.

"One day, when all our people were gone out to their works as usual and only I and my dear sister were left to mind the house, two men and a woman got over our walls, and in a moment seized us both, and without giving us time to cry out or make resistance they stopped our mouths and ran off with us into the nearest wood. Here they tied our hands and continued to carry us as far as they could till night came on. . . .

"The next day proved a day of greater sorrow than I had yet experienced, for my sister and I were then separated as we lay clasped in each other's arms. It was in vain that we besought them not to part us; she was torn from me and immediately carried away, while I was left in a state of distraction not to be described. I cried and grieved continually, and for several days I did not eat anything but what they forced into my mouth. . . ."

This drawing was made in England in 1799 and shows an unwilling civilian being taken by force from his family and friends by a navy recruiting party.

For most African slaves, life in the Americas was a nightmare of cruelty and hard labor. Poor whites from Europe who were kidnapped and sent to the plantations in the early days at least had the chance of making some money and gaining their freedom. African captives were normally slaves for life, as were their children after them.

Slavery was not abolished in Britain until 1807, nor in the United States until the Civil War of 1861-1865. Even then, the slave trade continued in other parts of the world. Arabs continued to abduct villagers from the Sudan and East Africa and sell them into slavery. South Pacific islanders were kidnapped by gangs and shipped to European-owned sugar and cotton plantations on the islands of Fiji and Samoa and in Queensland, Australia. Here they were sold into hard labor by brutal slavers known as **blackbirders**, such as the notorious Ross Lewin. These mass kidnappings began in about 1847 and were not finally stamped out until 1904.

PRESSED INTO SERVICE

While the African slave trade was at its height, many of the poor in Europe were being treated little better than slaves. For centuries, governments had forced people to serve in the army or navy. Naval officers would arrange for **press gangs** to roam the streets of cities. Men and boys would be seized, beaten senseless, and carried off. Prisoners would be snatched from the jails. They would awake with a sore head to find themselves at sea, enlisted in the navy. They could do nothing about their fate.

Conditions on board ship were horrific. The food was poor, wages were low and irregular, and the punishments included flogging, torture, and hanging. British naval crews were recruited by these official kidnap gangs until the nineteenth century. By then, two serious mutinies had forced the authorities to think again.

> Our fleets are defrauded by injustice, manned by violence and maintained by cruelty.
>
> *Edward Vernon,*
> *English admiral (1684–1757)*

During the nineteenth century and even later, it was still common for the crews of merchant ships to be kidnapped in a similar manner. Sailors would be tricked, drugged, or beaten in port and carried on board a departing vessel. They would be forced to serve as crew until the next port. American sailors on the clippers, the tall ships which sailed to China in the 1870s, had a name for the practice: to **shanghai**. The name came from the Chinese port of Shanghai, where such kidnappings were said to be common.

HELD FOR RANSOM

A tense moment during the TWA hijacking in June
1985. A negotiator approaches an armed hijacker on
the runway at Beirut, Lebanon.

Kidnapping in all its forms has continued into the twentieth century. It has been encouraged by war, uncertainty, and the extremes of wealth and poverty in many different parts of the world. Political kidnappings carried out by small groups of armed terrorists have hit the headlines. Other kidnappers have simply wanted ransom money. In many cases, the results for victims and their families have been tragic.

KIDNAPPING FOR A RANSOM

On May 21, 1927, American flying ace Charles Lindbergh guided his plane down to Le Bourget Airport in Paris, having flown 3,571 miles (5,760km) from Long Island. He was the first person to fly the Atlantic Ocean solo and won a prize of $25,000. Lindbergh was an overnight hero and he soon became rich and very famous. At this time many people in America were suffering from extreme poverty, and Lindbergh was envied for his good fortune.

On March 1, 1932, Lindbergh was dining with his wife, Anne, at their New Jersey mansion. Shortly after 10:00 P.M. the nanny found that Lindbergh's 20-month-old son, Charles, Jr., was missing. The baby's crib was empty. A ladder was found outside, and a scrawled ransom note had been left on the windowsill. It demanded $50,000, warned against publicity, and assured the Lindberghs that their child would be cared for. Lindbergh, in despair, arranged for the ransom to be paid as instructed.

News of the kidnapping shocked America. The press clamored for action. A search force of police officers and civilian volunteers was set up. Nearly 100,000 individuals were involved. When news came on May 12, it was tragic. A truck driver had discovered the body of the baby in the woods near the Lindberghs' home. Charles Lindbergh, Jr., had been beaten to death.

On September 20, 1934, a German-born American, Bruno Richard Hauptmann, was arrested for the

WANTED

INFORMATION AS TO THE WHEREABOUTS OF

CHAS. A. LINDBERGH, Jr.

OF HOPEWELL, N. J.

SON OF COL. CHAS. A. LINDBERGH.

World-Famous Aviator

This child was kidnaped from his home in Hopewell, N. J., between 8 and 10 p. m. on Tuesday, March 1, 1932.

DESCRIPTION:

Age, 20 months   Hair, blond, curly
Weight, 27 to 30 lbs. Eyes, dark blue
Height, 29 inches   Complexion, light
Deep dimple in center of chin
Dressed in one-piece coverall night suit

ADDRESS ALL COMMUNICATIONS TO

Copies of this poster were distributed and displayed on street corners in an effort to trace the missing Lindbergh baby. The case remains the most famous kidnapping of the twentieth century.

kidnapping. Police said that he possessed some of the ransom money that had been paid out. Hauptmann protested that he was innocent, and there was certainly little hard evidence against him. He was found guilty and executed at New Jersey State Prison in Trenton on April 3, 1936. Many still doubt whether Hauptmann was really guilty. They point out that anti-German feeling was very strong in the United States at the time and may have influenced the case.

The Lindbergh case was typical of the many criminal abductions that took place around the world in the twentieth century. Many of the victims were relatives of the rich and famous. In December 1973 John Paul Getty III, the teenage grandson of a famous millionaire, was released to freedom. He had endured six months' captivity at the hands of Italian kid-nappers. They had demanded a ransom of $750,000 and cut off his ear.

POLITICAL KIDNAPPINGS

Kidnapping has sometimes been used as a political weapon. In 1972, for example, car factory workers in France who had been fired for their political views took the law into their own hands. They kidnapped one of the company managers and demanded their jobs back in return for his release.

One of the most famous political kidnappings since World War II occurred in California in February 1974. Millionaire heiress Patty Hearst was seized from her home by revolutionary terrorists known as the Symbionese Liberation Army. She was taken to an unknown destination and locked in a cupboard. A tape was sent to her family demanding free distribution of food to the poor. This was carried out. The story took a strange turn in April of that year, when cameras recorded some bank robbers in action. One of them was Patty Hearst, carrying a gun. When she was finally tracked down and released, she said that she had been brainwashed by her kidnappers and had been forced to carry out this robbery.

This picture was sent to a San Francisco radio station. It accompanied Patty Hearst's taped announcement that she was joining the Symbionese Liberation Army.

In March 1978, this photograph of the kidnapped Italian politician Aldo Moro was sent to a large national newspaper. The banner in the background carries the name of his kidnappers, *Brigate Rosse,* or Red Brigades.

Sometimes kidnap victims are powerful people such as businessmen, lawyers, or politicians. On March 16, 1978, an Italian terrorist group known as the Red Brigades ambushed the car of the country's former prime minister, Aldo Moro. They gunned down his police escort and demanded the release of two Red Brigades members from jail. For weeks nobody knew of the kidnappers' whereabouts. The government received notes from Moro in which he pleaded for the terrorists' demands to be met. However, the Italian government decided not to give in. On May 9, 1978, Moro's body was found in a car parked on a Rome street. Four years later, 63 people went to trial for involvement in the kidnapping. It was one of many such incidents in the 1970s and 1980s.

HOSTAGES AND HIJACKINGS

The ancient practice of taking hostages continued during the twentieth century, but it was adapted to modern times. In 1948 a Catalina flying boat belonging to Cathay Pacific Airways was seized by Chinese bandits. It was flying to Hong Kong. This was the first recorded **hijacking** of an aircraft.

During the 1960s and 1970s hijackings became more and more common in all parts of the world. Innocent passengers on planes, boats, and even trains and buses were sometimes seized and used as hostages in an international bargaining attempt. On June 14, 1985, gunmen belonging to a group of Shiite Muslims based in Lebanon seized an American TWA airliner after it had taken off in Athens. They demanded the release of 700 Shiites being held in Israeli jails. Thirty-nine Americans on board were taken prisoner in Lebanon's capital city, Beirut. They were not released until June 30. The following day, the Israelis released their prisoners. In other political hostage cases, the bargaining and behind-the-scenes discussions have been even more drawn out, and hostages have endured many months and years in captivity, not knowing when, or if, they will be released.

STATE TURNED KIDNAPPER

Throughout the twentieth century, governments have used kidnapping as a method of achieving their aims. During the 1930s, the National Socialists ("Nazis") seized power in Germany. They allowed no opposition to their views and were violently **racist** toward Jewish people. Many Jews and many of the Nazis' opponents were kidnapped and murdered. Innocent people were seized and carried off to camps where they were either subjected to hard labor or systematically murdered. Official kidnapping of this kind became the policy of the Nazi state.

In the Soviet Union, many of the ideals that had inspired the Russian revolution of 1917 were lost or corrupted by the 1930s. Here, too, under the iron rule of Joseph Stalin, all criticism was silenced. Secret police stole people away. Their knock on the door at dawn was awaited with terror. Many thousands of individuals were carried off, imprisoned without a fair trial, sent to **labor camps** and psychiatric hospitals, or killed. The imprisonment of some was used to blackmail others into giving information. This, too, was a kind of kidnapping, but with the support of the state, it could be practiced very widely indeed.

> No government has the right to make people disappear.
>
> *Amnesty International,*
> *organization campaigning for human rights*

The use of kidnapping by governments has continued into more recent years. In South Africa and in parts of Central and South America the story has been the same. Governments, or squads of thugs paid by the government, have seized their opponents, locked them away, and tortured them. During the 1980s, the South African government tried to crush the growing political opposition in the African townships. Many Africans were arrested and killed. In

A young Jewish boy is seized by Nazi troops in Warsaw, Poland, in the spring of 1943. When the Second World War ended in 1945, many Nazis were tried for war crimes at Nuremberg, in Germany. The picture of this abduction was used as evidence against them.

1985, 800 schoolchildren were rounded up in the South African township of Soweto. Many of them were beaten and tortured by the authorities in an attempt to gain information or a confession. Some of these children were less than ten years old.

In Argentina, those seized by the military

In a 1983 demonstration in Buenos Aires, protesters show placards of their missing relatives, kidnapped by the Argentine military government in the 1970s.

government and its agents between 1976 and 1983 became known as "the Disappeared." These victims of official kidnapping simply vanished. The babies of women who had been kidnapped in this way were "given" to the wealthy families of government supporters who wanted to have children. Many never heard from their real parents again.

SPIES, AGENTS, AND DIRTY TRICKS
In November 1964 a group of important Egyptian government representatives, or diplomats, appeared at an airport departure office in the Italian capital, Rome. They had with them a large sealed trunk marked "diplomatic mail" that was to be sent to Egypt. Italian customs officials were amazed to hear cries coming from the trunk. They opened it and found a man who claimed to be a Moroccan. When questioned by police, it turned out that he was an Israeli-born secret agent named Mordecai Luk, who had been working for Egypt. He had been kidnapped at a café in Rome

the day before. The mystery of this case was never solved, for the Egyptians claimed **diplomatic immunity**. This meant that they did not have to help police with the inquiries. The Egyptian diplomats were expelled from the country.

A similar incident later shocked British customs officials. When President Shagari of Nigeria was overthrown in December 1983, his politician brother-in-law, Umaru Dikko, fled to Britain. In July of the following year Dikko was seized by kidnappers on the streets of London. He was handcuffed, drugged, and packed into a large wooden crate. An Israeli, Dr. Lev-Aire Shapiro, was packed into the crate with Dikko, to be his "minder." The crate was taken to Stansted Airport, where a Nigerian plane was waiting. Airport officials became suspicious when their dogs sniffed the smell of drugs from the crate. They called the police, who sealed off the airport and made several arrests.

These two stories surprised people at the time. However, the practice of kidnapping individuals who are living overseas and bringing them home for trial is not so very unusual. Many countries allow their secret service agents to do this for political reasons.

THE NEW SLAVERS
Most people believe that slavery is part of a bygone age, abolished long ago. Unfortunately it still exists in many parts of the world. Human beings are still bought and sold in parts of Asia and Africa and used as forced labor on farms or in workshops, as servants in homes, or as prostitutes.

Such practices are normally illegal today, but in many countries the law has broken down because of war, famine, or poverty. In the city streets of South America and India, for example, there are many homeless children who may be seized and abused without anyone noticing. They may be forced to beg or work for little or no pay, or they may be forced into prostitution.

FAMILY QUARRELS

Some kidnappings take place within the family. The kidnapper may even be a parent who has been refused custody, or the right to look after his or her own children, for some reason. Feeling desperate, this parent may try to take them from their home or school and run away with them, sometimes to another country. Such a parent may well believe that a "new start" is in the children's best interest. Even so, such kidnappers are breaking the law and very probably disturbing their children's happiness and security.

From the 1970s onward, the divorce rate rose dramatically in most developed countries. As more and more families separated, the number of the family abductions also increased. With partners of different nationalities, some tug-of-love cases have involved prolonged suffering for parents who lose their children to faraway destinations where it is difficult, if not impossible, to visit them. For the children there may also be a great sense of loss and helplessness.

KIDNAPPER AND VICTIM

A gunman holds a cameraman captive in a local television studio in Arizona. This kidnapper kept his victim at gunpoint for several hours and demanded to have his own statement broadcast on the air. This closed circuit television picture showed negotiators what they were dealing with.

Criminals who turn to kidnapping as a way of making money are playing a desperate game. They do not know how the victim will react in captivity. They cannot predict how the relatives will respond when they get the ransom note. Even if the ransom money is paid, the kidnapper may not know whether the bank notes have been marked in some way. A kidnapper faces many unknowns.

CRIMINALS UNDER PRESSURE

Huge numbers of police officers were involved in the search for the kidnapper in the Lindbergh case nearly 60 years ago. Today, the police have many more ways of trapping a kidnapper. With the help of computer records, likely leads can be followed up more quickly. Telephone calls can be traced with ease. Officers can plant bugging devices in rooms or on individuals. A **reconstruction** of the crime can be acted out on national television, which helps to jog people's memories. There are also instant communications with police forces in other countries.

The seriousness of a kidnapping crime, and the pressures of carrying it through, are sometimes so great that the kidnapper panics. This is very dangerous for the victim. It can mean that the whole exercise ends in violence and murder.

POLITICAL TACTICS

Terrorist groups who carry out political kidnappings face similar pressures. They, too, have to keep their own identities secret and make use of **safe houses** to hide their captives. At the same time, they need to make their demands known to the outside world. They need the support of others, either by frightening them into obedience or by gaining their sympathy for the particular cause. They may be up against army units as well as the police.

From the 1970s onward, the Provisional IRA (Irish Republican Army) used violent abduction as part of their campaign to bring about a united Ireland. They

Dear Sir:

      Proceed immediately to the back platform of the train. Watch the east side of the track. Have your package ready. Look for the first LARGE, RED, BRICK factory situated immediately adjoining the tracks on the east. On top of this factory is a large, black watertower with the word CHAMPION written on it. Wait until you have COMPLETELY passed the south end of the factory - count five very rapidly and then IMMEDIATELY throw the package as far east as you can.

      Remember that this is your only chance to recover your son.

      Yours truly,

      GEORGE JOHNSON

This ransom note tells the father of a kidnap victim how and where to deliver the ransom money — from a moving train. Even if a note is typed, like this one, it can still provide vital clues to police scientists.

kidnapped people to **intimidate** them by maiming and injuring them. They held people hostage while they made use of their cars or houses. They even hijacked motorists and forced them to carry bombs to the target area. The press refers to such victims as **human bombs**.

Many terrorist groups train their members as if they were soldiers, so that they treat their victims as enemies rather than as fellow human beings. The abductors of Patty Hearst called her a "prisoner of war." Her kidnap was referred to as an "arrest" and the murder of others as "execution." The kidnappers of Aldo Moro "tried" him in a kind of "court." They claimed to speak on behalf of the poor and the oppressed.

A WAR OF NERVES

Most governments declare righteously that they will not deal with terrorists. None of them wishes to, but political hostage-takers know that in the end governments may be forced to negotiate. There is usually a lot of pressure from ordinary members of the public to secure the release of innocent hostages. Aldo Moro died because the Italian government would not deal with the Red Brigades. However, some people would argue that a government deal could encourage further kidnapping.

Rescue bids are often dangerous and may place the lives of hostages in peril. In April 1980 a United States rescue mission crashed in the Iranian desert during an attempt to free Americans held hostage in the country. The United States later made secret deals with the Iranian government, but claimed that these were unrelated to any hostage issues.

The tactics of hostage-takers are to play a waiting game. The victims are held in close captivity for months or even years. The conditions of imprisonment are often appalling. However, the hostage-takers believe that in the end the political situation may change and a bargain may be struck.

At the start of the 1991 Gulf War the president of Iraq, Saddam Hussein, seized foreign citizens living in Iraq and Kuwait and detained them at key places where the allied forces might attack. They formed a **human shield**. Under these circumstances, bids or even full-scale attacks were impossible.

THE VICTIM'S EXPERIENCE

To the victim of a kidnapping, the terror of being abducted may be enough to cause serious harm. Whether the kidnappers threaten violence or not, the shock of being seized in a hijack, for example, may be

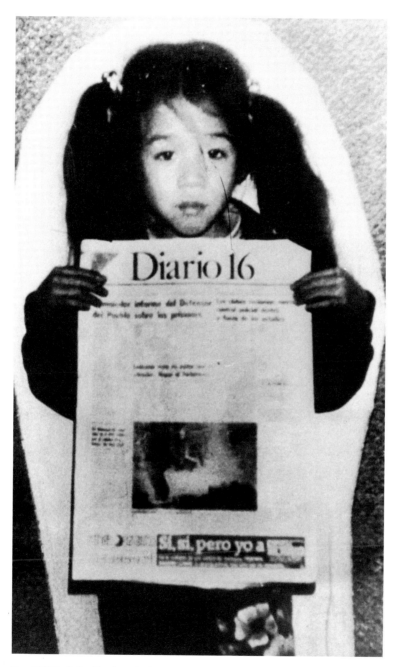

In 1987 this little girl was kidnapped on her way home from school in Spain. Her kidnappers demanded a ransom of $13 million and sent this photo of the girl holding up a dated newspaper as proof that they were holding her alive.

This nervous British boy was paraded on Iraqi television in 1990 at the side of the country's president, Saddam Hussein. The pictures were meant to show that foreigners in Iraq were being treated well, but when they were shown in the West, people were horrified that President Hussein's "guests," as he called them, were being held against their will in a country that was on the brink of an international war.

fatal in the case of an elderly victim with a weak heart. If a kidnapping lasts any length of time, the victim has to face all the conditions of imprisonment, as well as enormous uncertainty over what will happen next.

Many kidnap victims are forced to make statements or public appeals against their will. They may be refused food, water, or medicine until they do so. They may be forced to answer questions, beaten, or tortured. They are often kept in isolation, away from other people and without any news of the outside world. The kidnapper is unlikely to tell them where they are being held, in case this information can be useful in an escape attempt.

Even under some of these conditions, kidnapped prisoners have been known to form friendly relationships with their captors. In a political kidnapping, prisoner and guard may discuss the political background and reach greater understanding. However, the atmosphere always remains uncertain, since there are no rules of conduct governing an illegal kidnapping.

SURVIVAL AND SUPPORT

Human beings are capable of surviving the most terrible experiences. Many victims of kidnapping have shown amazing strength and bravery. They have marked the days of their captivity off, one by one, to record the passing of time. They have found ways of smuggling out messages to the outside world or of communicating with other prisoners. Some have even invented small games or mental puzzles to help them keep their minds active and sane.

> The secret of surviving in these conditions is to live for the day. . . .. Disappointment is so crippling.
>
> *Moorhead Kennedy,*
> *American hostage in Iran, 1980*

Perhaps the hardest burden that the abducted person has to bear is separation from friends, relatives, and fellow countrymen. Without this human contact and reassurance anyone can become depressed. The victims can lose confidence. Even their belief in themselves can be destroyed.

The ordeal may be just as horrific for the relatives and friends. While the kidnap is in progress, they imagine the victim being injured or killed. They feel that they are helpless. Should they rely on the police or the government to secure the freedom of the kidnap victim? Should they take any action themselves? If the victim has been kidnapped by soldiers or armed gangs, how do they find out what has happened to them? The strain and the responsibility are enormous.

When hostages are seized overseas and held captive for long periods, the friends of the victims often organize public campaigns to ensure that they are not forgotten. They may pressure their government to take action to secure their release. Hostages who are released from captivity are sometimes able to pass on information and encouragement in these campaigns.

On April 17, 1991, 10,000 London taxicabs flew yellow ribbons from their aerials as a mark of respect for the missing British journalist John McCarthy, who had been kidnapped five years earlier in Beirut. The custom of tying yellow ribbons around trees or wearing them on clothing began in the United States.

Jill Morrell, leader of the campaign to release British hostage John McCarthy, ties a yellow ribbon to keep his memory alive. McCarthy was finally released in August 1991. His kidnap ordeal in Lebanon had lasted over five years.

An overjoyed crowd welcomes American hostages back to New York in 1981. They had been held captive in Iran for 444 days. Once they are freed, many hostages have to cope with publicity and questions about their experience.

The ribbon is a symbol of homecoming and hope for a safe return. It is now used in other countries by supporters of kidnap victims and hostages.

RELEASE AT LAST

When release comes, the kidnap victim suddenly becomes aware of the outside world once again. There are **press conferences**, interviews, and journalists asking questions. There may also be questions to answer from police officers or government officials. Then there are welcoming ceremonies and joyful homecomings.

However, freedom rarely marks the end of the

ordeal. Kidnap victims may be scarred for life by their experience. They may be physically injured or disabled. They may suffer recurring nightmares in which they recall their captivity. They may become fearful of public places or activities.

It is very hard for kidnap victims to pick up the threads of their former life. Some have found it difficult or impossible to concentrate on their work. In other cases long separation from loved ones has strained relationships. Abduction can shatter the whole world of the victim and it may prove very difficult to put the pieces together again.

> ...even I
> regained my freedom with a sigh.
> *From "The Prisoner of Chillon"*
> *by Lord Byron, 1816*

HELPING HANDS

Fortunately, in many developed countries there are organizations that can offer advice, or **counseling**, to the victims of kidnapping and other violent crimes. Experts can help individuals and families come to terms with past events and face the future. They can offer practical advice regarding medical attention or government assistance.

DEALING WITH ABDUCTION

A woman suspected of a baby-snatching is being taken to a local hospital. Her face is covered to hide her identity. Some kidnappers may be confused, desperate people who need medical help.

In 1982 the Red Brigades, abductors and killers of Italian politician Aldo Moro, were finally brought to trial. Antonio Savasta, a former member of the Red Brigades, is seen here giving evidence in court.

The first weapon against the crime of abduction is the force of law. In most countries of the world there are laws against kidnapping, with sentences varying from imprisonment to execution for those found guilty.

In many countries laws have been made as a result of particular cases. After the Lindbergh kidnapping of 1932 the laws of the United States made kidnapping a national, or federal, offense. Anyone found guilty of carrying a kidnap victim across a state border could face the death penalty. Later laws were passed to ensure that the FBI (Federal Bureau of Investigation) would be called in after 24 hours of any kidnapping investigation.

LAWS AGAINST POLITICAL KIDNAPPERS

The United States Congress has defined political kidnapping, along with hijacking and hostage-taking, as terrorist crimes. With the increase in such crimes in recent years, many countries have passed special laws to tackle the problem of terrorism. Many lawmakers feel that the police and courts need special powers to combat terrorists.

Other people believe that the existing laws can deal with any problems that might arise. They argue that a government will not defeat terrorism by using terrorist methods itself, but by keeping to the rules of international law. Some claim that anti-terrorist laws passed in Britain since 1973 have contributed to the problems in Northern Ireland rather than preventing them.

> Where laws end, tyranny begins.
>
> *William Pitt,*
> *English statesman (1708-1778)*

INTERNATIONAL AGREEMENTS

Many kidnappings and abductions take place across national borders. Even when countries have good relations with each other, their laws may vary. They have to come to an agreement concerning legal matters.

Without a clear-cut agreement between countries, those guilty of abduction may escape justice. In October 1985, United States aircraft forced down an Egyptian plane carrying a Palestinian terrorist. He had been involved in the violent hijacking of a Mediterranean cruise liner, in which an elderly American hostage had been murdered. The plane landed in Sicily, an island which belongs to Italy. The

Italian police insisted that the American forces had no right to make an arrest on Italian soil. They took the Palestinian into custody and later allowed him to leave the country for Yugoslavia.

WHO CATCHES THE KIDNAPPERS?

The fight against all kinds of kidnapping requires tight security at ports, airports, and railroad and bus stations. Security guards, coastguards, and airline officials are on the lookout for anything unusual, and members of the public have often come forward with vital clues in well-publicized kidnap cases.

Each country must decide which forces to use against which kidnappers. If the police are called in, then they must decide whether to use a local unit that knows the area well, or a national unit that has wider experience. In practice, both are often required to work together in the search for a kidnapper.

Many national security forces have special military units trained to deal with hijackings and hostage-takings. Units such as the British SAS are trained in unarmed combat, marksmanship, hand-to-hand fighting, and taking possession of buildings during a siege. In 1980 the SAS launched an attack on the Iranian Embassy in London, where staff had been held captive for six days by a group of gunmen. Nineteen hostages were rescued and four of the five gunmen were killed.

Many kidnappings and hostage-takings end in a siege. The captors are surrounded by police or army forces. They threaten to kill the hostage if attacked. Under these circumstances a different approach may be necessary to save lives and to bring the kidnappers to justice. A **psychologist** may be brought into the case. This expert may advise a slower approach in which the captors are spoken to or delivered food. After several days the captors may become tired and confused. They may then be overwhelmed in an unguarded moment or persuaded to give themselves up.

British SAS forces storm the Iranian Embassy in London in 1980. The hostages being held at gunpoint inside were rescued. Using force is a high but sometimes necessary risk taken to end a kidnap situation.

CRIME PREVENTION

Laws and police action are necessary to deal with crimes once they have taken place. However, campaigning, educating, and counseling may all help to reduce the likelihood of kidnapping taking place in any of its various forms. International voluntary organizations such as Amnesty International can draw the attention of the world to countries that encourage abduction. They have already spotlighted the plight of "the disappeared" in countries around the world. Social workers and psychiatrists may reduce the stress that leads to acts of violence such as abduction. Government publicity campaigns can alert parents and children to the possible threat of strangers to unattended children and babies.

QUESTIONS OF RIGHT AND WRONG

Most people would agree that kidnapping is evil. Nobody wishes to be captured and detained against his or her own will, and so nobody should capture and detain another human being in the same way. The rule of law is surely the best protection against such abuse.

As always, however, there are areas in which these issues are less clear. If the laws are made by a state that is itself unjust, should they be obeyed? When European countries were occupied by the Nazis in the 1940s, the German authorities took hostages from among the local people. The hostages were held captive and killed if there was any trouble in the region. In return, the local people took any opportunity they could of abducting and murdering German officers or civilians.

RELIGION AND ABDUCTION

Surprisingly, perhaps, people claiming to be religious have always been among those guilty of crimes of abduction. The Englishmen who founded the Atlantic slave trade worshiped in church each Sunday and received Christian burial. In Northern Ireland, Protestants have abducted Roman Catholics and Roman Catholics have abducted Protestants. In Beirut, the troubled capital of Lebanon, Christian and Muslim groups have been involved in abduction and hostage-taking.

Despite this sad state of affairs, the scriptures of most of the world's religions explicitly forbid the theft, greed, violence, and deception that accompany

Kidnapping thrives where there is poverty, and where law and order have broken down. This eight-year-old orphan from Bogotá, Colombia, is just one of thousands who are open to attack on the streets of the world's poorest cities.

kidnapping crimes. Christians were in the forefront of the battle against the slave trade in the last century and are still prepared to lay down their lives in the cause of justice. In 1980, in the Central American country of El Salvador, a Roman Catholic archbishop, Oscar Romero, was gunned down because he condemned the kidnappings and murders carried out by supporters of the government.

THE FUTURE

History has shown us that abduction is an ancient fear and has been a continuous problem over many centuries. However, history has also shown us that the crime can be combated.

For centuries, the rich sons of powerful families could seize peasant girls and engage in abduction, false captivity, and sexual assault without being brought to justice. For centuries, orphaned children could be kidnapped and put to work. These are now crimes with severe penalties. The struggle to create laws that would protect the weak against the strong was long and hard, but it was effective in many parts of the world.

However, there is still a long way to go before every country in the world commits itself to providing basic human rights for its citizens. In many lands, laws regarding abduction are ignored by the authorities. They may turn a blind eye to slavery or forced labor. They may lack the money and resources to enforce the law or to pursue the kidnappers. In times of war, law and order may break down completely. These problems all need to be tackled in the struggle against kidnapping and similar crimes.

KEY DATES

3100–332 B.C.
Abduction in Egypt: Seizure and enslaving of neighboring peoples such as Hebrews.

1000 B.C.–A.D. 476
Slavery in ancient Greece and Rome: Buying and selling of slaves in the marketplace, many abducted from their homes in northern Europe by raiders.

400–800
The breakdown of law: Piracy, raiding, abductions common throughout Europe.

1193
A king is ransomed: Richard I of England kidnapped and handed over to the Emperor Henry VI, who demands a high ransom.

1212
The Children's Crusade: Mass kidnapping of young pilgrims bound for the Holy Land.

1513
Abductions in the New World: Slavery introduced into the Americas. Abductions of Native Americans by Europeans.

1650s
Stolen from the Guinea Coast: Mass abductions from West Africa as the Atlantic slave trade increases.

1670s
First use of term *kidnapping*: Abduction of English youths to plantations in Virginia and Barbados.

1700s
Abductions by press gang: British navy recruits sailors by seizing men from ports.

1755
The Equiano case: Kidnapping of Olaudah Equiano, sold into slavery.

1847
The blackbirders: Start of mass abduction of Pacific islanders for enforced labor in Australia.

1870s
Shanghaied! Merchant seamen attacked and carried on board departing vessels.

1932
The Lindbergh case: Classic case of criminal kidnapping of an individual.

1930s
Reigns of terror: In Germany and in the Soviet Union, mass abductions into forced labor and death camps.

1948
Kidnap in the air: First recorded aircraft hijack. A Cathay Pacific flying boat going to Hong Kong is seized.

1970s
Political kidnapping: Heiress Patty Hearst and former Italian premier Aldo Moro among many kidnapped by political terrorists.

1990
In the firing line: Foreign hostages used as a "human shield" against attack in Iraq at the start of the Gulf War.

GLOSSARY

abduction: Carrying off or kidnapping of another person.

baby-snatcher: Someone who seizes a baby from a public place.

blackbirder: A term once used in Australia to describe slavers who sold Pacific islanders into forced labor.

counseling: Helping people through the discussion of their problems and the offer of useful advice.

diplomatic immunity: An international agreement that prevents diplomats from being charged with crimes when serving overseas. They can only be sent back to their own country. The agreement has allowed several people to escape from charges of abduction.

hijacking: Violent seizing of goods or people in transit.

hostage: Someone who is held against his or her will until the captors' demands are met. A hostage may be held for many years.

human bomb: Term used by the press to describe someone who has been abducted by terrorists and forced to carry a bomb into a targeted area.

human shield: Anyone who is placed in a dangerous position by a captor. The idea is that the hostage protects the captor from his or her enemy.

intimidate: To frighten someone in order to make them do something.

kidnapping: To seize or detain any person illegally. The term originally referred only to the capture of children.

labor camp: A detention center where people are forced to work excessively.

press conference: A meeting at which journalists are given information.

press gang: A group of sailors used to carry off people and force them to join and serve in the navy.

prostitute: Somebody who engages in sexual intercourse in return for money.

psychiatrist: Somebody who treats mental illness.

psychologist: Somebody who studies the workings of the human mind.

racism: The belief that there are differences between the human races that make one superior to another.

ransom: A sum of money or other reward paid in return for the release of a captive.

reconstruction: Acting out the events of a crime after it has occurred, in the hope that witnesses may remember important details.

safe house: A secret hideout that is safe from attack.

shanghai: To overpower a merchant seaman and force him to join the crew of a ship against his will.

terrorist: Person trying to bring about political change by illegal and violent means. Terrorist methods might include kidnapping, hijacking, arson, bullying, murder, or causing explosions.

tug-of-love: A term used by the press to describe disputes between separated parents over who should care for their children.

INDEX